Psychic Experiences
of
An Indian Princess

Daughter of Chief Tommyhawk
(Mrs. Annette Leevier)

Published by
THE AUSTIN PUBLISHING COMPANY
LOS ANGELES, CAL.

TO SITTING BULL—THE SIOUX BRAVE.

Oh, Sitting Bull, to you I say
   Come close to me and always stay;
That I may know you're ever near,
   And knowing it I'll never fear.
Let your judgment and wisdom rule
   In me—an ever ready tool—
To give your dictates to mankind
   That men the light may ever find.

Oh, Brave, in all your pow'r and might,
   Come unto me both day and night,
And in your power let me stand
   An instrument shaped to your hand.
That through your power I may find
   The means of helping all mankind,
To ope my way by voice and pen
   For blessing to my fellow men.

FOREWORD.

Since facts, no matter how prepared, clothed or presented, are the stepping stones and guiding stars to truth, light and vision, this work presented in the following pages is but a stepping stone for those who may desire to grasp, or those who are grasping—the spiritual principles linking the past and present in a homogeneous ascendancy to that wonderful future and supreme hope—life after death.

The work is incorporated as an autobiography consisting of two parts, the first dealing with events in my life while in the convent, and the second, with experiences as a medium and healer. No notoriety is expected, or inflated statements recorded; but, a presentation of the truths—heretofore tabooed and retarded by the hands of opposition and prejudice—which have occurred as personal incidents or achievements in my life.

An apology is necessary to the reader for not recording a more detailed account of my life. Owing to the circumstances of my early life—living within the perpetual darkness of convent walls—days, months and years passed in a monotonous procession, marked here and there with incidents unforgetable, which are stated in the work.

If the reader has any antipathy toward Spiritualism and challenges the veracity of the statements in this work, I would be pleased in every instance to give the names and addresses of the anonymous persons mentioned. The reason for preserving and withholding the name is simply a question of deference. People concerned—if living—might object to the use of their names, hence, I have taken the alternative of merely telling the incident but reserving the right of supplying the correct names.

Lastly, Spiritualism withholds nothing—and emphatically demands the truth and nothing but the truth—hence, if this work attracts and causes some sensible-minded individuals to see the light where darkness has heretofore existed, and furthermore causes them to enter circles—the doorway to spiritual unfoldment and knowledge—in pursuit of further enlightenment, the effort spent in preparing this work will be well compensated.

PART I.

From the available but vague and scattered family records handed down by word of mouth, or through the memory of recitals of glorious deeds and suffering hardships, I am able to give but a brief sketch of my ancestry. But brief as it is, I value it for that reason the more. My grand parents were in America and took part in the early wars between the English and French settlers of Quebec—now a Canadian province.

My grandfather on my father's side was known as Big Sun of the Pontiac branch of the Mohawk tribe; Pontiac being a very prominent figure in the very early Indian Wars for possessions of lands. My grandmother was known as Princess Laconquinne of the Ojibwah tribe of Indians.

The mother side of the house came from Bordeaux, France. My grandparents—leaving France because of the Revolution—sought temporary refuge in America until peace had been restored. While in the midst of preparations prior to returning to their native land, fire broke out in their home and destroyed all their earthly possessions. This made it necessary for them to remain on this side. They never saw their native land again in the material life.

Father was born in Quebec in 1836, and was called Sunnie, because he was born in the early morning about sunrise. He was of the Ojibwah tribe of Indians. This was due to frequent intermarriagees of the Ojibwahs with the Mohawks—his father being a Mohawk. His education was purely Indian, being specially well versed in the use of herbs. As he grew older he became such a scrapper that he was nicknamed Chief Tommyhawk—after a famous predecessor.

He lived amongst the Ojibwahs until he fell in love with a young French girl. This brought trouble, because the parents did not approve of the pact. Leaving their homes, the young couple eloped and were married in the Roman faith—my mother being a good Catholic, but my father being a believer in the Great Spirit, never entered a church in his life.

I first saw daylight in Quebec, being born, as I was told later, with a hazy veil over my face, regarded at that time as a sign of wisdom. I was also possessed of spiritual powers, being born with such an intensely sensitive organization that I responded to the necessities of the time and became an instrument in the hands of higher intelligences long before I fully realized my gifts, and much longer before I was able to fully reason the why and how of them. Often rappings were heard in my presence in the evening, and mother had to awaken me to quiet the spirits. These were the cause of mother's interference, and caused the suppression of all my efforts in telling people interesting things.

As a consequence, I received a Convent education. At three years of age I was put into the hands of the Sisters of the small community Convent, to be raised and taught religion. When of proper school age, I was sent to Notre Dame in Montreal, at which place mother had arranged and paid for my tuition and care, until I was prepared to become a matron or a nurse or take the veil. Choosing the latter when the time arrived for a decision, I took the white veil. It was a sane course to take—as I thought at the time—for my mother had departed from the material life and my father had married again.

After a time I became restless, nervous and in general, feeling ill,. besides being very anxious to know more about my new mother. Receiving permission, I paid a visit to my father's home. It took but a short time to learn the bitter truth—that I was not wanted. Knowing that the time had come for a change to other scenes and conditions, I went to bed in that house for the last time during the visit.

While in bed I felt myself taken out of the body and seemingly made to float through the atmosphere and space. I know not how long I remained in this condition, but on my return to the body I sought father. After a long talk and argument, it was decided that I would either have to return to whence I came or go to New York.

Choosing the latter, arrangements were made whereby I was transferred to New York to another Convent to work out my own salvation. One afternoon—the day preceding the anniversary of my birth—I again seemed to be taken out of the body. This time I spent the afternoon—as we call it—in visiting another planet to witness what you would term "Life after Death." Not being quite able to understand these transitions, they became a source of worryment to me, more so on this particular day.

My duties now became varied between matron, nurse, and housekeeper, and through all this my first love affair developed and progressed. My greatest earth hope and lover was a priest, but as we were not allowed to speak, we enjoyed thought communication in its elemental form. During a sickness which proved fatal to him, I became his nurse in company with an associate—the rule being that we must always work in pairs under such conditions. While on his deathbed, he promised faithfully to return to me. Being mediumistic, he believed in spirit return.

As time passed I became restless and worried, for my lover had not returned to me as he had promised. I had hoped for greater changes, and had looked forward to frequent visits from him from the spirit side. But to think of entering into a new year without him was perplexing to me. My whole soul cried out to him, and I prayed for him to hasten the time when I could come to him.

Early in the afternoon of a hot summer day—the 4th of July—I heard the beautiful strains of the Rosary. Following this a great change seemed to come over me, a drowsiness and a longing to get to my cell and lie down. As I came to my door on the way to carrying out my desire, I saw a misty, shadowy form standing outside my cell, apparently awaiting me. I crossed the sill, turned and locked the doors and laid down on the couch.

The physical senses became dormant almost immediately, and a sinking sensation ensued, followed by the casting off of physical limitations—a tearing sensation at first—causing a sudden expanding feeling, bringing joyousness and the new thought of freedom. The freedom of mind brought on the intense desire for knowledge. With avidity the mind had adjusted itself as a finely, sensitively attuned instrument, to respond to the thoughts of spiritual beings— to hear, see, and learn that which only higher spiritual intelligence can accomplish and teach.

The door quickly opened and someone stepped into the room. Moving hurriedly to the side of the couch, and reaching out his hand he demanded that I go with him. Casting my eyes up, I recognized him—the object of all my affections—the one to whom my heart had been crying out. My prayers seemingly were answered. He said, "Come, as I desire to keep my promise."

He did not appear to me just as he had been in the body. His face had undergone such decided changes—appearing so much brighter than I had been familiar with— that I could scarcely look at him. A long loose robe covered his body. He did not appear to walk on the floor, but to tread on air. When I arose and took his hand neither of us seemed to walk but to glide onward and upward. On looking back, I saw my own body lying on the couch apparently in slumber, but in reality awaiting my return.

We seemed to rise through ceiling and roof out into the air, in line with and over the great cross on the spire. Looking down, we could see a wonderful panorama of the city and its people—a criss-cross myriad of finely woven webs of street intersections, blended and mingled with the glittering sun rays merrily ricochetting from New York's watery boundaries. Soon this was lost to view, for we traveled inconceivably fast.

Looking about, I became aware of the fact that we were nearing what appeared to be another plane or planetary sphere. I asked, "What do you call that place?" His answer wafted to me like the soothing murmur of a zephyr, "Home of your Soul." Looking, I first saw a most beautiful river. On crossing this water, it appeared to be more white than blue and so tranquil and placid that not a ripple could be seen anywhere. Beyond this a tropical country scene unfolded itself to our view. This view made me think that this entire plane had been carpeted with an over-abundance of grasses and flowers—the grasses appearing a greenish blue color. Tropical ferns seemed to abide everywhere. Oh, it was beautiful and delectable to behold. Everything we looked at appeared possessed with a diamond lustre, but in reality only the brillance of dew drops. Stars and colors were prominent and intermingled at all points. The fragrance was inspiring and odoriferous. There was nothing of a harsh nature to be seen, everything being of that harmony one would expect to find in our spirit or eternal home. There was nothing to greet my ears but the soft murmur of voices linked with that beauty and sweetness which can only come from a heavenly sphere.

After allowing me time to view this heavenly condition, we sailed on and came onto a view of a beautiful city. I can give but a faint idea of the construction of the same. No tall buildings were visible; all evidently of a uniform order. These abodes—for such they obviously were—were strangely fashioned with no roofs and of one color—white.

One in particular that I was attracted to was an exception in magnificence and splendor, and unusually large compared to those in the vicinity. As we approached there appeared to be a large veranda covered with flowers and vines of every description; but no steps to any part of this house were discernable. We came closer. I could see no one but could hear the rapturous strains of music and soft, cooing murmur of voices within. As we listened, it seemed as if elaborate preparations were being made for some special ceremony. Some one came to the door and said, "Come, for the feast is ready." It evidently had been prepared for me.

I seemed to feel the presence of relatives and friends within, especially that of mother. I started to go in but my guide checked me, saying, "You must not enter there, for I have orders to take you on with me." As I turned it seemed to me that my loved ones felt my presence, for a great desire came over me to stay. You can readily know how I felt when I was told that I could not stay with them. To relieve the condition they did not come into view. I asked of the guide what it meant, and he replied, "If I allow you to go in there I could not get you back." He was right, for had I met and seen mother he never could have persuaded me to leave. I would have sacrificed all in my power to have stayed there.

I worried and grieved very much because I could not have my own way, but he knew beter than I. My soul's desire was to go to mother or to keep him—my guide—with me, but my time had not come for that end. My mission on earth had not been completed. If I remain true to my trust and my spirit appointments and work diligently, I shall receive my reward in the future. When the time comes he will return for me and then there will be no more separation.

Allowing me another view of the big city, he turned me on our homeward journey. We stopped nowhere, having overstayed our time at the one particular place. Slowly we ffoated back toward our own earth plane. On our way, I seemed to be returning to a dark prison or vault. On approaching closer to our earth the din of noises and confusion, the rumble of traffic greeted our ears—at first but faint but increasing in crescendo until it became a veritable profaneness. It was a hard task to reconcile myself to the consequences and the accompanying feeling. I could but recall the following words:—

"Weary of earth and ladened with care
I looked toward heaven and longed to be there."

Being in bondage and trying to repent that great, quiet under-way of living, and at the same time trying to worship God, a fearful chill came over me and seemed to repulse me completely. I felt I could not enter my house of flesh. Before entering my cell, I pleaded earnestly to return with him. He only allowed me to wrestle with him, but I clung so tight to his robe that he came in with me and waited until I had regained my earthly consciousness, giving me the charge that we both should know the truth, and that he would soon come and take me on another flight or soul excursion. To my surprise, I found that I had just enough time to attend to my duties, having been out of my body for five hours from one o'clock until six o'clock.

After that flight or soul excursion, I have never felt as though I belonged to this earth or plane, always wanting to turn away from here and go home, for it is the home I'm preparing for myself on this material plane. In a message sent me sometime later through another medium, he said,

"Marie, I am awaiting you over on the golden shore where parting comes to us no more, where eternal happiness awaits us. Safe with me, for I love you best of all; you are my choice and I rejoice; then, in our happy home never more to roam alone you will become my loving wife. H. T."

Several months later I was shocked to hear the sad news that father was dying. Receiving permission from my superiors, I returned home for the last time. He lingered but a few days. During his dying moments I stood at the foot of the bed, and as if in a dream I saw father leave his body, rise into the air, transform and come back to earth as a spirit being.

At the funeral while the prayers were being said, a knocking was heard. The neighbor friend next to me tiptoed to the front door, but saw no one. Again the knocking was heard. This time the woman went to the back door, but again found no one. I never spoke a word, thinking to quiet the spirit in that way. That it was the spirit of my father, making a noisy protestation against the prayers being offered over his dead body—he not being a church member, but a believer in the Great Spirit and spirit return—is true without a shadow of a doubt. After the funeral, I could hear him meandering about with that same old dragging, shuffling step. At one time noises were heard emanating from father's former bedroom. On investigation no one was seen, but I soon understood for I remembered that a "strong-box," covered with metal sheeting, in which father kept all his valuables and important documents, was in the room. He had evidently been knocking against this sheeting. The reason I did not enter the rooms frequented much by him was that it was only a signal for him to begin his knocking My sojourn in this room was of the shortest possible duration, soon returning to New York again to resume my former duties.

At another time while sitting under a tree in the Convent in meditation, I heard music. It seemed to be above me in the tree, of a weird, far-away tone quality. I looked up but saw no one. I knew no singing was allowed at that hour, yet it came louder with the rustle of the leaves, so clear, so strong. I knew in an instant it was no earthly music, for I felt as though no earthly voice could render such sweet song as that, as on my ears these gracious tidings fell, "Believe and confess—thou shalt be loose from all."

I then looked up. Laying aside my Rosary that I always had carried and had placed such confidence in, I began to rejoice with the heavenly hosts. As I did so, I heard the most delightful string music sounding like that of a harp. It increased in volume until it reached a tremendous climax point, and then I recognized that hymn of hymns—"Rock of Ages." In full melody it seemed to vibrate through all things in my surroundings. I did not recognize any of the voices as belonging to any one I knew who had crossed the divide. In a little while the strains of music left me, taking with them my longing to follow and my lingering gaze. I saw nothing; I could only hear these words, "Blessed is he who believes but does not see."

Before entering the house, I read the II. Samuel 22:2, "The Lord is my rock and my fortress." Then I arose perfectly content and went in, realizing we walk by faith and not by sight. I was so content that I took only what the spirit world gave me, feeling sure sight would come later. The environment and unconscious sway of influence these intelligencies had over me made it impossible for me to question what the ultimate result of it all would be.

I did not get back out of doors again in a long time to visit that beloved spot under the tree. Having overstayed my time that evening, I had to undergo a light punishment. I sat a watch in my own room and sang. While singing, "Jerusalem, Hark, the Angels Sing"—to my surprise came the music on the harp as an accompaniment. A few moments later all left and there came a reaction and calm. Being disgusted and discouraged with the turn of events, I had had enough experience inside of those walls, and should lay plans for my escape.

> A nun sat in her prison cell
>   Doomed all the days of her life,
> And her thoughts went out to the beautiful world,
>   "Will I never be free from this strife?"

> A songster sat on the window ledge
>   And the poor girl's heart was stirred;
> "Just follow me," it seemed to urge,
>   To the Convent sang the bird.

I became so useful in my life as a Sister that I was trusted with a visiting list so often that I was practically privileged to go about wherever I pleased in New York. I not only went where they sent me, but also where I was not expected to go—listening all of the time to my spirit guides, and going wherever they took me. I—Indian-like—desired to roam from one scene to another, appearing sometimes at places where I had no business being. There seemed a condition surrounding me, such that I never tried to avoid anything I came in contact with. No matter where I went I could always see or feel Big Chief—my father—close to me watching that no harm befell me, and I never felt any uneasiness. Many times as I wandered on in deep thought, I would hear his voice calling me to take care and give attention.

I frequently came in contact with poor, down-trodden men and women, who would appeal to me for help and financial assistance. Very often 1 gave up half of what I had previously collected from patrons on my visiting lists. Many times I went to the homes of the poor and the criminal, and what I saw would make me heartsick. In some I found intoxicated men and women so low down and degraded that there seemed to be no possible help for them; in others all stages and descriptions of diseases wre present; while in others crime and filth were the outstanding features. Many of these people were out of the daily prescribed route, but that made no difference to me; I did all the good I possibly could.

One day I passed by a large prison. On looking up I saw Big Chief standing, looking at me, and he said, "Here is work for you to do." "But how can I get in?" I asked. The next day, as I passed the same prison, I saw a poor, careworn woman who stooped and asked for prayers, also begging me to say a prayer for her son who was incarcerated within. I was only too glad and willing, and availed myself of the opportunity.

Following the poor mother, we were allowed admittance. I talked to the son and prayed for him and bade him read a small Bible which I left, and which he took with him to Sing Sing prison. Having an opportuinty to follow up the career of this young men, I later learned that the seed I had planted had yielded fruit.

I did not think it wise to tell my superiors what work I was doing. By doing this 1 had better opportunities to carry out my plans. There was a great longing in my breast to see Coney Island—New York's amusement park—by night, for I had heard so much about it.

Making my plans accordingly, I walked out the back door one evening and down the garden to the wall. Under my arm was a box with a rope in it. At the wall whom should I see on top but Big Chief—my guide. Below him I saw notches in the brick wall by means of which I was soon over the wall. On the other side I found a good thoroughfare for making my way without attracting the attention of anyone, to the home of a friend of mine with whom my escape had been prearranged. In a short time I was properly attired and my friend and I set out for the park. How I enjoyed that lark no one knows but myself. I came face to face with many I knew but they, seeing me in civilian clothes, did not recognize me.

I was forced to spend the night with my friend, as it was not feasible to attempt to return at such a late hour. Coming back early enough in the morning, I passed through the Church saying my prayers. When asked where I had been I replied, "Out on a little mission." The Mother Superior thought different and started in to box my ears, but this was one of the times I would not submit. Reaching out, I tore the veil from her head and she just barely escaped with her life, for I was so furiously angry that I was tempted to throw her over the railing and down the stairs. The sentence and punishment meted out to me was the maximum imposed for such offences.

On my way to the cell for punishment I was met by the cook who stealthily handed me a lunch, for she knew I would get nothing all day. This I secreted until I had been locked in. Then I took time to eat and enjoy a small chicken, and amongst other things a flask of wine.

While eating, a shadow passed through the door and there before me stood Big Chief. He flashed a spirit light about the cell so that I could see where I was. He showed me a vision of the assassination of President McKinley; several war views, one of them fought under palm trees, while in the other red-coated soldiers were engaged; an earthquake; and a stream of roaring water predicting floods. He knelt beside me and pleaded with me to leave the place we were in and to trust myself to his guidance, for he would take care of me. Then a vision of mother came—weeping because she had left me in such bondage.

I vowed to follow Big Chief and confide in the Great Spirit. Going to the door—with my guide—I found it unlocked. I went about my duties as if nothing had happened, trusting all the time in my guide. When my superiors saw this they hurriedly made arrangements for my transfer to Philadelphia.

Thinking to get rid of me, I was sent from Philadelphia to Newport News, Va., where an epidemic of yellow fever was raging. But all to no avail, for I took up my duties as a nurse and gave what succor I was capable of, withoua being protected in any way from the disease. I realized later what danger I had submitted myself to, but only received greater faith in my guides. When my work at this place had been completed, I was sent back to Philadelphia to assume my new duties there.

I found quite a few mediums among the priests and nuns. On recollection, I don't wonder at the above statement. For what is more desirable for spiritual unfoldment and attraction to the Great Beyond than to be shut in from the noise of the busy world, surrounded by flowers, music and incense and of necessity—concentration on devotion.

Unconsciously or subconsciously the gateway is opened, bringing joy for the discovery of the newly found truth but disappointment for the environments and servitude chained to them during their physical life.

Psychic phenomena were demonstrated daily. The Sister Superior often interrupted my associate Sister and me while we were enjoying thought transference with both the living and the dead—for no other reason than that she herself was psychic and knew of our pastime. Of one particular instance I remember where the spirit of my lover—the priest—brought me thoughts from a priest in Cleveland who was to figure prominently in subsequent events. While this side of the experiences was roses, the thorns presented themselves in as much as we had to be guarded in both active and subconscious thoughts, and in our actions, lest the psychic Mother Superior get acquainted with everything about and between us.

I had been ailing three weeks with a rheumatic attack which affected my left limb, when an interesting incident occurred. Coming down the stairs very early one morning to prepare the lights for early mass, I felt weak and faint, making it necessary for me to support myself on the railing. Suddenly a crescent about two feet wide appeared at my feet. I stepped onto it with my left foot and immediately a light flared up. Frightened, I ran up the stairs and down by another, to perform my duties; but the ailment had left me. Several years later the spirit of Moonbeam—came to me with a light and crescent, and I then realized that Moonbeam had cured me of my rheumatic attack.

About this time I began to listen to my spirit friend in his effort to have me give up this bondage and go out into the world to see and do what I could. After due consideration of all things concerned and connected with my proposed flight, I told the Sisters. This created quite an excitement amongst them. They threatened, scolded, cajoled and promised, but all to no purpose, for I had had a glimpse of what was in store for me, and determined that my relations with them must cease. They sent urgent messages to the heads in Montreal, but this made no impression on me. The orders from Montreal were to hold me to the vows I had taken, and promised me a better home for the money my mother paid for my tuition and care.

Fortifying myself against all or any possible conditions that might arise—knowing that an authority from Montreal would likely arrive any time—I went quietly into the last prayers of my career as a nun—one night. While kneeling before a life-sized crucifix, and all sincere in my devotions, I heard a great crash, and instantly following this, Big Chief appeared before me, accompanied by the spirits of my mother and of two Sisiters I had known in life. They stood side by side until I had finished and then they faced about and in single file passed through the door. By impulse I followed them out. As we passed the door, I went into the Church proper where I saluted and paid my respects to the fourteen stations of the Cross—representing Christ on his way to Calvary; also paying my best and most loving tribute to the Madonna for a special prayer in my behalf. When the great outer doors closed behind me, freedom was mine.

At that moment the thought came, "What shall I do?" The exultation, the new air, the quickened, unknown heartbeat, the desire to shout to all the world the news of my freedom—all descended upon me so quickly that I was completely confounded. While I was pondering and thinking over how I had previously arranged my plans, a bird twittered and finally broke into a song. It seemed to be a message of love and encouragement to me; it seemed as if the birds were even interested in my case.

Recovering my mental equilibrium, I hurried to my friend's home—the one who had escorted me on the Coney Island escapade. After a hurried explanation and consultation, she gave me some civilian clothes to wear on my fight. Further cautioning and urging her to keep my fight from the priests' ears, I departed, feeling somewhat easier in the acquired attire.

Having some means I went to the station and purchased a ticket for Cleveland, Ohio. At this place I found old friends and neighbors of my father's who were sympathetic with me in my flight and with whom I rejoiced in my newly acquired freedom. For a whole day I remained indoors still wary lest I be apprehended.

The following day we started on a shopping tour to outfit a wardrobe for myself. While busily engaged in talking and viewing the sights while passing from one store to another, I espied a priest coming towards us. In passing, our eyes met, and I knew I had been recognized through the medium of higher intelligences, and by means of powers acquired through unfoldment and environments—as referred to previously. I acquainted my friend with the news, at the same time telling her I would journey to another point.

That night I took a boat to Detroit. In the morning I hunted for a desirable room—finding one, about noon time. The relaxation, the cold, cheerless four walls surrounding enclosure and the future outlook made me despondent. There I was—unwelcomed—a fugitive in the eyes of the world—trembling, nervous, blue, downhearted. Do you wonder, gentle reader, at my condition? My thoughts were as nervous as I physically was . They agitated me in a comparison of the past—the quiet life—with the then present—dodging, unhonored, unrespected career. In this brooding state of mind I passed the whole of the afternoon.

In the evening, I lay down all worn out. I immediately became aware of the fact that I was not alone. I closed my eyes and instantly saw the shepherd—my priest—standing close by saying that he had given up his life for his sheep. He had his crook in his hand and two small lambs in his arms. He came so close that he touched me, saying, "It is the songs you sing and the smiles you wear that makes the sunshine glow; also, may every morning seem to say there is something happy on the way." Jumping to my feet in a dazed condition, I cried, "I am ready—take me now." I had not stopped to think; this I realized when I had recovered fully. I knew I was not ready, for there were many things not yet accomplished. My mission on earth really just had its beginning. But before I had arrived at a worthy end I could not expect the longed for journey across the divide to join my loved ones. To Jesus I said, "My sorrow sets too deep for this life to look for peace and happiness from anyone but you. Human sympathy is too shallow as a rule, so I must look higher and say,

'Thou does't remember,
Midst all the glories of Thy Throne—
The sorrows of humanity,
For they were once Thine own.' "

In the morning restlessness returned to me. I later received a visit from Big Chief who bade me follow him. My destination under his guidance was Walpole Island—the Indian Reserve. While there I sent word to the Mother Superior at at Philadelphia and the priest in Cleveland that I had sought refuge among my ancestors' people, and had further denounced all creeds and joined the Great Spirit worshippers. Also, during my stay, I attracted the Spirit of Pontiac—the great Indian warrior and trailer.

The following day I retraced my route to Detroit again. On returning to my place I found that I was not alone, for the Spirit of Pontiac was my companion. He came to me as a shepherd to watch over me, as I was one of his lambs, and to teach me to trust in him.

He took my soul on a journey to develop within me the desires of my spirit loved ones for my education that was to fit me for my lifework. He showed me the great peaceful river; he took me a long distance over green fields and towns and finally stopped at a large, beautiful fountain where he bade me drink. At another stop he invited me to a great feast. Oh, what joy there seemed to be among the people over the return of Big Chief Tommyhawk with a brother from earth life who was to remain with them. I could not see him—Tommyhawk—but I felt his presence. This feast appeared to take place in the open and under the protection of a hill.

We then visited with Princess Laconquinne, my grandmother on my father's side—who sat at the entrance of a magnificent white palace. She evidently was mistress of the place, which apparently was a haven for mothers. I was then piloted through a long dark valley. A light was visible in the distance, at first a dim ray, but brightening as we neared the end. At the end I was met by my spirit guide and returned to the body. As evidence of their faith and watchfulness, I received the following poem.

There's a fair Indian maid
   Whose duties are laid,
On the banks of a beautiful river.
With her guides, their lives never sever.

Her duties are plain
   As they sweep through the brain,
Their love for her so exceeding,
   Revealing to her their presence so near
As they touch her when gently kneeling.

The Physical plain oft causes a pain
   When absence is felt when she wanders,
But oh, what joys
When she hears from her boys,
For she feels they are always about her.

These brave Indian boys
   Were always her joy
When oft on the trail they did wander,
   Ever mindful of her and the pleasures she seeks,
Ever watchful that. love will surround her.

Her desires for good
   Are all understood
By the braves that give her power;
   Make her life very dear, with their presence so near,
And always on watch to defend her.

Entering on the second phase of my career—which appears to be a reincarnation to do worldly good—I have myself wondered and marveled—on retrospection—at the absolute power of the unseen forces. My lifework had been cut out for me; chiseled, irremovable on the marble pillars of accomplishment. My guides—the spirits of the known and unknown to me in this material life—being parties to the conspiracy to effect my escape, gave birth to the desire within my mind—nursing it in characteristic fashion until the psychological moment had arrived for the smouldering in my breast to break out into a seething flame. The turn of events which made my freedom possible is but another instance of their handiwork. Once free, I was further directed on my course. I do not lament; I only wonder and try to surmise what I will be called upon to do next; I am ready, at all times under all conditions.

Being prepared and ready to do the bidding of my spirit guides, I failed to keep as accurate and as detailed an account of my later life as would be necessary for a work of this type. Consequently, the work under this part is not recorded in a chronological sequence, but under headings of the various topics such as Healing, Trailing, etc., which gives in a synopsized form, an account of my experiences and accomplishments. Even the various cities and towns—there being so many—are not mentioned in detail. I belong to various state organizations, but I always undertook volunteer work, never waiting to be called upon by the associations. Arriving at one destination and completing my mission, I was either invited or guided to another—usually within a short radius. Using one of these places as a headquarter, I worked out from the same—in this manner covering quite an extensive territory. I've made no commercial issue of my talents, just taking and receiving remuneration with my traveling expenses plus my upkeep.

My guides, who have striven to render invaluable aid to alleviate some of the perplexities of the material life, are all Indians with the exception of two—my mother and H. T., the priest.

H. T., my priest, is my personal comforter and guide, helping me at all times and teaching me of his world and what I have to look forward to in the future life.

Mother—is the receptive guardian—the gatekeeper for all spirits who desire to communicate with me.

Tommyhawk—my father—for self-protection and for those I ask of him to battle for. In true Indian style, he comes accompanied by his six dogs which have materialized in a materializing circle.

Sitting Bull—Tommyhawk's companion at times.

Princess Laconquinne—my grandmother on my father's side—for message work.

Two Indian children—who help in circle work.

Moonbeam—my Indian medicine-man who helps me in

my healing.

Pontiac—the trailer and locator for the hidden or the lost.

Of these guides, the first three mentioned were known to me in earth life, while the remaining were attracted at some previous time. I can depend on my Indian guides not to give false or misleading statements because in earth life an Indian despises the man with a crooked tongue. Further, they do not throw the condition of their passing out of this material life over me. Examples of what they have accomplished through me and my talents are given under the following articles:

HEALING.

In a peculiar yet simple and logical manner my success as a healer can be comprehended. My father was known among the Indians for his knowledge of herbs and the manner of compounding simple remedies—crude in most ways, yet common-sense, practical Nature in themselves. These necessary requisites in physical structure and properties were mine. My hands are soft, cushiony, and warm, allowing the vital magnetism to be directed outward, drawing the blood with it. Then thru psychometrical work I am able to locate the center and base of the ailments, making it possible in many cases to do away with all experimenting.

In my work in this branch, I have learned fundamental points which—if the doctors were to follow more closely—would compensate both doctor and patient. Of the greatest importance is the diverting of the patient's mind from the ailment. This accomplished, I gently touch the afflicted parts and with low words of assurance offer suggestions, but being tactful to have the patients follow me throughout all. For some I pray and have them pray. Where music is advisable I have it played or sung. But of all, I take greatest care to await impressions to do the healing—not at any time but only when encouraged and aided by my spirit guides.

While traveling from Detroit to Sandusky, Ohio, in answer to a call from a circle and to help the resident members to the best of my ability, the spirit of Moonbeam—the Indian medicine-man—appeared before me. He informed me that there was work to be done and that he would be with me throughout the entire period.

He was right. On appearing on the rostrum, I found that I could not go on with the scheduled message work. Going down into the audience, I walked down the aisle and was guided to a certain woman whose name I don't know. I felt my arm; there was a pain. "I hurt myself by falling out through the doorway with a washtub," I told her. Much to her surprise and chagrin, I took her arm and gently massaged it. My statements were correct, for she admitted that she had hurt herself in the manner stated. Being a poor woman who washed for a living, I was heartily pleased with my work and thanked my guides.

At another time while there, I undertook to cure a case without personal contact with the party. I stood on the rostrum and in answer to my guides said, "There is a certain party by name of Henry—a lawyer—who has an injured wrist and whose father also tells me that he is skeptical about our work." The man's wife raised her hand and verified my statements. "He hurt his wrist while out on a hunting trip and while carrying a gun," I continued. They also acknowledged that. I told him to remove his wrist band and give me a good thought. I rubbed and treated my own wrist and prayed for him, knowing that the spirit of his father was doing likewise with his. I was informed later by his wife that he had never worn the wrist band again and that his views on the subject had been revised considerably.

By means of massaging and the prayer cure a crippled woman was somewhat relieved. She had been unable to walk without the aid of a crutch for three years, and the last five months preceding the treatments she had been in bed. After three treatments a relaxation of the muscles was effected and since then the woman has been able to walk with the aid of a cane.

People are skeptical of such versions as stated above. In Columbus, in a circle, a doctor—receptive to a certain extent but still a doubter—brought in a paper on a difficult medical case where exact diagnosis was lacking. By means of psychometrical reading, I was able to locate the exact center and base of the ailment. He became very enthusiastic and wanted to know why he, with all his university training and technical knowledge, had to be told by one who had no diploma, nor had seen the patient. Then he became acquainted with the fact that everyone is psychic—some very much more so than others. The requirement to develop the hidden powers within ourselves to attend circles and try to unfold. This power is but dormant in some people, and like a stiffened member of the body, needs exercise, it needs but attention and patience. The doctor became an enthusiastic member of the circles I held during the year I was there.

TRAILING.

In my work under this heading, my guide, Pontiac, figures conspicuously. While working—recuperating from the exhaustion brought on from the healing cases—Pontiac came to me and said, "Tell your neighbor that her son is not lost. Tell her to go to Coldwater, Michigan; visit a man there by the name of Ames who runs a barber shop, and he will tell her where to find her son Les." This I did and she became highly excited, for she said that she had been awaiting an opportunity to ask if I could help her in locating her "lost boy." Following my instructions, she brought the "boy" back home with her shortly before Christmas and was able to enjoy the first happy Yuletide in the twelve years of his absence.

Another lady hearing of the above by means of some devious channel, as news of this character travels, came to see me about her son. Pontiac told her through me that her son had gone never to return home to settle down. He further added that she should go home and call on the Great Spirit every day until he brought the son to her from Huntington, Indiana. During the interval preceding the young man's return, I sat under the sunflowers—at the back of my lodging—at twilight, and kept in touch with the spirits of the young man's actions. At the end of three weeks, the prodigal son returned for a visit to his home in Freemont, Ohio.

Shortly after this, while at Amherst, Ohio, a man from Republic, Ohio, came to see me. Before he had made the object of his visit known to me, Pontiac told me to say, "Your mother has the money, that's why you no find. Go to your home in country; go to spring house where you keep milk; look down deep in mud under water-trough, and in a cream jar you will find 500 wampams ($500.") He did so, and found the amount as stated. The father and mother of this man had quarreled. Following the disagreement, the mother had hid the money but had died before telling her son where to find it.

In a case of this kind, locating treasure is permissible. But I have emphatically nothing whatever to do with seeking or helping others to locate treasures that were acquired unlawfully and then hidden. The spirit condition guarding the treasure is anything but satisfactory. Should the treasure be found, the visitation of bad luck, failures, and apprehension will soon deprive the finder of his ill-gotten fortune. Death is a very common gain reaped by such treasure hunters.

A case of this character was enacted in the vicinity of where I was staying, Pontiac explaining to me the cause of it all. Four young men had stolen some money, and in their flight, one of their number was killed by pursuers. The money was buried by the remaining three in a thick woods. One night one of the three attempted to crawl up and get his share of the booty. He was shot and killed by one of the others who happened to be lying there unknown to the first young man. A clear instance of the earth-bound spirit of the first killed wreaking havoc on the other three by causing one of their number to die the death he did.

Pontiac guides me clearly enough in such cases. His work is only to do good for humanity. The instances as stated give but a few examples of the work he had helped perform to relieve a few of the many aching hearts.

TITANIC PROPHECY.

Three days before the Titanic went down to its watery grave, I had a vision of the disaster, but did not get it clear enough to distinguish a ship, nor the place of the accident. The evening of the fatal night, while sitting by myself I felt a feeling of unrest and weariness coming over me. Giving way to my feeling I prepared to retire, but before I was even comfortably settled, I saw a shadow cross my eyes. Looking up, I saw Big Chief and a Hindoo member of his band.

They talked together for a few moments, and immediately after their conversation I felt myself drawn toward them. It seemed as if we were floating above the ocean. Looking off into space, we could see what appeared to be a large floating palace. As we approached, it seemed to take on all the colors of the rainbow—a picturesque object. When we came closer to it, its appearance changed to that of a large, beautiful butterffy—a winged personification of gayiety and supremacy. It sped on and we watched. Suddenly it seemed to disappear between two walls of ice and snow—we lost it. On coming to my senses, I was wet from sweat, cold, and frozen from the effects. Several mornings following, the world received the news of the great marine disaster.

SOUL FLIGHT.

Following shortly after the Titanic premonition, the spirit of Tommyhawk—my father—came to me. "It is time to take another flight to the ethereal planes," he told me. Having no control over my physical body when in his hands, I could but obey his instructions. In a few minutes I felt my soul leave the body and we went up until I became hopelessly lost.

At this time I seemed to hear father speak to me; he bade me look. As I looked in the indicated direction, the most beautiful castles came into view. On approaching and entering the doorway, we were enveloped by the inky black which seemed to hang on every side. The corridor was with apparently no sidewalls. On the far end we met with the extreme opposite; a flood of glistening sunshine greeted us.

The view afforded at this juncture was delectable to behold,. Within a magnificent wigwam, sat Princess Laconquinne, my father's mother. On seeing father and me, she gave us a great welcome and took me inside of the wigwam. When we went in I was astonished at the transformation, for instead of seeing the interior of a wigwam, as I had expected, I found that I was within a spacious, awe-inspiring palace. Within, forest flowers and fruits abounded, while without, a placid stream flowed very gently on— a picture of love and peace, purity and wisdom. We walked or floated side by side for what seemed hours until she halted and bade me eat of the fruit which appeared to be cherries; but they were very large and juicy.

While eating she pointed off into the distance and said, "There is the Happy Hunting Ground of the Indians." There seemed to be no end to the hosts of people on the banks of the river. All were busy on missions of import, coming, going, making visits, always smiling; always on the watch for the arrival of some loved one from the earth plane who had not come as yet; always clothed in such garb as would easily be recognized by those just coming over the divide. In place of the customary war implements, they all carried musical instruments of various kinds, together with flags and other ornamental trimmings. While looking on this ostentatious display, music of the sweetest harmony seemed to surround us.

I turned my eyes toward the river, which was full of brightly painted canoes, going and coming. I asked Princess Laconquinne what was going on and why all these people seemed to be preparing for some royal event. As we talked a canoe came into sight; as it approached it looked as if it had turned into a beautiful palace floating in the ethereal air, fully decorated with flags and feathers of all kinds and of variegated colors. As it approached the shores someone said it had the soul of one who had just departed from the material life. I thought of the joy of the meeting, but could not see or hear what was taking place about the newly arrived soul. I expressed a desire to come home in the same manner, but Princess Laconquinne told me that was only used for spirit purposes. She then led me back to where Tommyhawk was patiently waiting for me. He in turn guided me back to my body. As I watched, I saw him step into his canoe and while gliding away heard his voice singing so sweetly, "Yes. we'll gather at the water that leads to the Happy Hunting Ground."

WAITING

Loved ones are waiting yonder,
  Over the Crystal Sea.
Oft do we hear their voices,
  Calling to you and me.
Oft do we see their shadows
  Oft hear the still small voice
Making our hearts feel lighter,
  Making our Souls rejoice.

Oft do we hear their music,
  Music of heavenly strain,
Naught but a voice from Heaven,
  Could sound that glad refrain.
Soon they will come and take me,
  To that dear Home on High
Where all is bright and happy
  And sweet welcome Bye and Bye.

Zimran is lingering near you,
  Filling your soul with love,
Teaching the path of duty
  Leading to joys above.
Oft, yes, oft do we grieve him
  When heed we not his voice,
But if we do his bidding
  Then does his soul rejoice

Angels all robed in beauty
  Stand near the open door:
Oh, will you bid them enter,
  Cheering us more and more.
Stars from their home are shining
  Over each path of woe,
Trying to lead us upward,
  Pointing the way to go.
Dear Ones, why tarry longer?
  Choose the right path today;
Let your face beam with gladness
  For those across the way.
Zimran is calling down to you
  And He will bring the key,
In all His truth and grandeur,
  Unlocking the Mystery.

TIFFIN PROPHECY

While resting one evening in my room by myself, prior to holding a circle Big Chief came to me looking sad. He vanished from my view and another form came into view, that of the warning spirit. He stood before me clothed all in white, a trumpet in hand, a sword laid across his breast, and very angry—his face very expressive. I arose trembling. l saw great bodies of water gushing in torrents; I saw houses, people, and animals floating by. I fainted and lay in this condition for some time.

Recovering my senses, I called my class around me and made the prophecy that Tiffin, Ohio would be under water within a short time. When the Mayor heard of the prophecy, he notified me that Tiffin tolerated no such folly and that I either had to leave the town or be subject to arrest. I sat down to look matters straight in the face; I surely had not expected such a reception from the city officials. It was discouraging—but just for a moment to know the truth—but have the populace decrying your statements as false, nonsensical and undesirable. While pondering as to my future course, Pontiac and Captain John Smith appeared before me. They held a jury trial over me—the jury consisting of the unseen forces. The verdict was in my favor; I remained in Tiffin until a few days before the flood. Knowing my vision was to befulfilled, I went over to Fostoria, Ohio. The great Angel went with me and drawing his sword he divided the city so that l knew where to seek refuge from the impending danger.

The flood came—the flood of 1913—that damaged or sideswipped every city, town and hamlet that bordered on a stream or river in the Ohio River basin. On returning to Tiffin—after the flood had reached its crest and had begun to recede—I found that six bridges had been swept away and ruin and devastation left in its wake. As I stood on the banks of the river, my messenger—the bird—came to me and sang a slow mournful song which spoke louder to me than a human voice.

Searching parties were busy seeking the bodies of all persons reported missing. They were successful in finding all with the exception of one—a Mr. Axline. Big Chief and Pontiac both came to the rescue and searching parties following my instructions were able to locate and recover the body. This was another triumph for me—the people having begun to believe a little when my prophecy on the flood had been fulfilled. To cap the climax, I told a woman—who had been made a widow through the flood—where to find her husband's gold watch.

Later on I made another prophecy that Tiffin would be somewhat damaged by a severe storm in the fall of that same year. To my gratification, the news was received by the people in a totally different manner from that which the flood prophecy had been treated.

Following my prophecies, I received further evidences from spirit friends who are at work at all times in conneceion with the human race, ever ready to send forth their messages of love to us. These were received on various occasions while quietly sitting—with my eyes closed—about twilight time. The name given at the end of each message is that of the spirit who transmitted the message to you through me and my guides. At the command of Princess Laconquinne to write, I received the following:

"Working out our own salvation,
  Firm and patient day by day,
Clearing thorns from each one's pathway
  Keeping enemies at bay,
No one far or near is slighted.
  Drop a line to each one here,
Never let one go unnoticed
  Banish every doubt and Fear."
                    —Martin   Luther.

"While gazing in the great beyond
  And asking if my friends are there,
The answer comes and lo! anon
  There comes a music on the air."
                    —Longfellow.

"Nothing ever pleases better
  Than to soothe the suff'ring one.
Let them know the Learned Healer
  Still on earth he can appear."
                    —Alice Bennette, Cleveland.

"It's only one more day, tonight,
  A message to you I did write,
Courage loved one you are right,
  Remove the cross out of your sight;
This spirit world is what we see
  They took the cross away from me."
                    —Martin   Luther.

"There came to me a guiding star,
  It fell to floor. It came I know not where;
I looked it o'er, 'twas made with care,
  A lov'd one's hand had placed it there.
A star in your crown you have won,
  You have toiled for Christ from sun to sun;
There's no reward on earth for this,
  The Master does not pay in gold."
                    —Abraham Lincoln

"Beyond the pearly gates I stand,
  A manuscript in my left hand;
What e'er you do both right and wrong
  I'll weigh it out and put it down.

Your judgment comes just once a year,
  In this same month when you were born
You'll realize if you have passed
  And entered in a better class.

Your teacher is the Master, dear.
  His life you've taught without a fear,
Those little ones brought near to Him
  And older ones with faith in Him."

Being near to my birthday, when I received the above annonymous spirit manifestation, I was greatly alarmed for the reason that no spirit name was given. This is regarded by mediums as an upbraiding for some wrong we may have committed or the omen that we would be censured even to the point of having the Holy Spirit send the summons to cross the Great Divide.

TRIBUTE FROM CHIEF TOMMYHAWK

Muche heape Good Man too
  Gave my country for His sake.
All I do for Great Spirit too,
  Fighting battles for all of you;
We are warriors brave and bold,
  We have no fear for our souls,
We know Him who gave us birth,
  He'll take care of all on earth.
No more our quarrels do we fight,
  Only your earth plots to make right.
Muche heape spirits bright,
  Draped in feathers all in white.
Robes white too, our faces fair,
  Are blessings sent to you so rare
By sitting Bull your comforter.
  Our wigwam doors are open wide
And he is constant by your side;
  I never leave you now alone
Until this long life's battle's won."

OBSESSION AND SPIRIT CONDITIONS.

Why I never married can be again attributed to the unseen forces. On becoming a nun, I was married to the cross and to those sacred vows. After laying aside the sacred veil and after those massive doors had closed me out into the noise contaminated world to go at will, the cross haunted me. Naturally enough, many times I sat and pondered over my escape, and thought of the cold convent life. To be all alone in this world was enough to bring on moroseness; to be compelled to learn the ways of the wicked world at such a late period in life was distasteful; to think of being forced to make my living, to make my new acquaintances, to learn to travel, was distracting. Taken in all, the predicament I found myself in—without the aid of the superior beings—was unenviable. But trusting to my spirit guides, they blazed the trail for my journey in life up to the present, and have made the life that looks barren to the uninformed bystander as pleasant as they have seen fit and necessary.

But the idea dawned on me to have an earth companion as well as a soul mate. It was embarrassing to me to have to wander onward over this earth's surface without a protector and guide. Again I felt the result of being shut in from the world. What must I do? That was my problem. I had enough admirers through the work I've accomplished to choose from. Was it up to me to make the initiative? Well, I made my individual attempts to fulfill my desires, but my guides were instrumental in frustrating my plans.

My first selection was a gentleman who had been an altar server in a Catholic Church. We were acquainted, and as far as I could comprehend certainly loved one another. Our plans for our future were maturing. We were to join another church of my designation, and also to have a happy, comfortable home. But before the climax of our simple love affair was attained, we had a disagreement one evening. As lovers generally do, we began to spat. Suddenly a light appeared in the doorway—peculiar, shimmering, and similar to that of a small gas flame. It came between us and then faded away. We both observed this phenomenon; we could spat no more. He asked an explanation of me, but I was too dazed at the time and offered none. He left me but we were never the same lovers after this visit from the spirit who protected me—there being no one on this earth to do it. Later my guide simply told me that my suitor and I could never have agreed, so I had to forget.

Another gentleman with whom I became great friends was in the navy of this country. I found great pleasure in his company until the day the crisis came. I knew it and felt it. I went with him to visit on the battleship Delaware —before it had been officially accepted. On going down the stairs while on this warship, I saw my spirit guide standing at the foot of the stairs. Then I knew the worst would come. Right enough, we disagreed over an insignificant topic before we left the ship and never made up again.

In another and last instance, the gentleman was a brother of one of my most intimate lady friends. We three spent many a happy time together, and I felt sure my spirit guide wouldn't interfere between us. But finally the long awaited day arrived. While we were walking the Board-walk of Atlantic City, I met my spirit and knew the end was near. Later on he went to work with the engineer corps on the Panama Canal. Since the time of his departure I have heard but once from him.

I was disappointed at the outcome of my love affairs, but thought over the reason behind these failures. I found that the spirit of the priest—my lover while in the convent and my conductor on the soul flight—had obsessed me, and had been the guiding influence. It was not his desire to have me become married. He had previously promised me that after I had fulfilled my share of work allotted to me, I would find happiness with him across the Great Divide. As further evidence from him to urge me onward, I receiv-ed a poem from him, counselling me to obey the heavenly voice.

OBSESSION

Obsession has given me unlimited food for thought. The subject is so large, so expansive and engrossing that vol-umes upon it could be written. But in the short space allot-ted in this work, it is hoped that the statements and refer-ences will cause the reader to desire more knowledge of same.

No one who is obsessed by a good spirit can go into bad company or commit evil; it won't allow you to. It's easy to attract a good spirit if we understand spirit return and obey the laws set forth by those who are capable of doing so. Unless the gateway—the inclination to resist with the in-domitable strength of higher thoughts and aspirations the influences of a lower nature—is open, such influences of a lower nature cannot enter as obsessing forces. That's why I wish everyone would concentrate; we are all psychic; not only the mediums but everyone. Thoughts are things—living things—therefore give out your best thoughts toward everyone and nothing but good comes back to you. By do-ing so we cannot attract an evil spirit wandering around on earth—commonly called the devil—who may have left the body under peculiar circumstances, and who may induce others to do likewise.

Have you ever stopped to think that through obsession a cause can be found for innumerable crimes committed, for the hosts of suicides and maniacs? The organization of the obsessing force must be similar to that of the obedient obsessed being. Realizing this and knowing that a spirit enters the spirit world just as it left this, there must be an innumerable host of low,uneducated, and evil spirits about. Hence if the obsessed party offers a deficiency of will power—weakness in control of their individuality—the gateway is open for an evil spirit of a harmonious organization—with that of the obsessed to enter. The ensuing result is a heartbreaking chapter of evil for which inevitable retribution must be received.

Think of those who give themselves to drink. One drinking man came to me while I was in Sandusky, Ohio, to ask me to help him. I said to him, "You have the spirit control of a man who passed out while intoxicated." "Yes, I know it," he replied. "We were both out fishing some twelve years ago in Sandusky Bay and became drunk. The result was that the boat capsized and he drowned. In going down the last time he yelled, 'I hope you drown.' Since that time I've been a drunkard. Whenever the thought of that drowning man comes to me I have to go in and drink. Furthermore, I neglect my family and their suffering makes me feel wretched when I'm sober."

I told him how to "brace up"—how it was possible to throw off his spirit condition. I had him come often; I prayed for him and gave him a prayer that he had at hand and repeated at any time the desire for his former debauchery seized him. I impressed on his mind the necessity of concentration on keeping straight—the fact that he still possessed will power and that he had to trust in it. In following up this man's case, I found that in obeying instructions, his home life had as a result been revolutionized—from a heart-broken to a happy state of existence.

Many spirits in similar instances of souls transient have obsessed the living person to live out the time they should have lived in their own house of flesh. In the above example, the spirit of the drinking partner had been back here on earth using this man's body just the same as if the body had been its own.

Spirit enlightenment of "earthbound" spirits can be accomplished by having them enter a circle. The spirit of Stanford White was in this terrible plight until I brought it to light. This spirit followed me for a long time, but didn't try to obsess me because he was too busy guarding Harry K. Thaw—his murderer—and keeping him in prison. I was holding a seance in Columbus, Ohio, when the spirit took hold of me. I was under control and tried to fight; I was so angry that I had to be held tight by those earnest sitters until the strife was over, and the spirit of his mother had joined him. Then came calm. Then he said, "Now that I'm with mother I cling no more to this earth. My desire is to get away if I can and Harry K. Thaw can go free." This was before Thaw's freedom for the sitters made note of the message and watched the newspapers. Within a short time—less than a year—Thaw's escape was announced and at this writing he is still a free man. The spirit of White has returned many times to thank me for uniting his spirit with his mother's. Had this spirit not been enlightened, it may have wandered on earth until it had attracted some weaker person and had made them die as he did.

Those gunmen of New York—who paid the penalty with their lives in the electric chair—also came in spirit, asking prayers, so that they, too, might get away from this earth—having passed out before their time had arrived. But such is in our life. The spirit missionaries, the spirit friends, and loved ones are incessantly helping those terribly hypnotized "earthbound" spirits from their lowly cycles on the upward path to the love that is ultimately awaiting them.

No wonder enmity and war never cease—whether individual, family, commercial, state, or international—once a start is made. There are more spirits fighting than human beings in any strife. As an instance, while conducting a circle in Cleveland a short time after Senor Huerta's—the former Mexican President—demise from earth life, the spirit of my guide Pontiac came and told me that Huerta was busy at the time fighting for and aiding that faction that had been his while he was Dictator.

If people knew what they were made for they wouldn't cause so many heartaches of others. But they don't understand the life they live and pass out to the Great Divide without knowing why and where they are going.

> Honor those whose words or deeds
> Thus help us in our daily needs;.
> And by their loving overflow
> Raise us from whate'er is low.

CONCLUSION

In summing up the story of my life, the question in my mind, dear reader, is not that of the past, present and future of myself, but for you and your future. I have been educated by my guides to prepare myself for the future—the real life and to know that the purpose of the physical body is the evolution of the spirit. In all history we find record of where our departed loved ones say to us, "If I only could have known of the beauties of what was in store for me, how I would have made greater effort to be more prepared for what was to come." So you can see, my friends, that even as we are, they do not forget to send us a knowledge of what their surroundings are. Every effort of theirs is for our betterment, trying in their way to guide us not only to a better knowledge of our own lives and conditions, but also of theirs. If nature should forget to produce her part where would we, as a people, be in a short time? But as you know, all things are provided for, and if we do not get what we want, it may be because our spirit loved ones do not think it best for us to have it. The trials of this life are only the purifying crucible we must pass through to make us understand our condition, and when all seems darkness and gloom, we are only coming to the purer light and condition of our real life.

And, if those we mourn as dead, live and love us beyond the shadows, we should not be content with bare facts; the more thoroughly we are convinced, the more eagerly should we avail ourselves of every opportunity to converse and receive messages. Through messages, they teach us that after death there is an immortal state, blissful, enjoyable for those who have led a good life on this earth, but dark, gloomy, abyssmal for those whose lives were stained.

Are you going to live a true life, or are you going to live a life of mockery? Will you live for Truth and Knowledge, or will you live a false life in the face of all sacred Truths and Principles as laid down? Will you live for a future life, or will you only live for the present? Will you live for our fellow man and woman, or will you live for mere selfish gain, ignoring all pretenses to goodness only to find after years of fad and fashion your life laid bare on the rotten shore of discord and discontent? Your answer and the faithful toil of abiding by your choice—dear reader— seals for you the future fate which all must meet, each one for himself. The Keeper can't be bribed. He doesn't pay or receive with gold but with Love.

Believe in th Golden Rule, "Whatsoever ye would that others should do unto you, do ye also unto them." Analyze your own character, and know you are above reproach, then practise the above and your lives will be in the care of the higher spirit powers. Don't give up in despair; remember that they will help you when you need help, providing you are deserving of it. In closing, I hope this small publication and others that will follow will touch some heart that is looking for peace and comfort from the spirit side and help guide them in some manner so that all will be found in the knowledge of a happy future and belief in the Great Spirit.

Sometime not far in the future
  Where the evening shadows play,
You'll watch the beautiful sunset
  And the power of sin fade away.

And as you sit in the twilight
  Dreaming of youthful hours,
The angels will come from heaven
  And strew your path with flowers.

But soon the glorious sunrise
  Will illuminate your soul,
And angels will come from heaven
  To gather you into the fold.

CPSIA information can be obtained
at www.ICGtesting.com
Printed in the USA
LVHW071616220722
724187LV00002B/11